Beyond Riches

Mastering Wealth for a Fulfilling Life

Collins Morgan

Table of Contents

Introduction

In the vast landscape of personal finance, the pursuit of wealth often conjures images of opulence, financial portfolios, and tangible assets. However, in the pages that follow, we embark on a transformative exploration that goes "Beyond Riches." This book is not merely a guide to accumulating monetary wealth; it is a roadmap to mastering wealth for a life that is profoundly fulfilling.

Redefining Wealth

At its essence, wealth extends beyond the realm of material abundance. It encompasses a tapestry of experiences, relationships, personal growth, and contributions to society. To truly master wealth is to understand that it is not just a destination but a dynamic journey that intertwines with the very fabric of our lives. It's about realizing that wealth is not an end in itself but a means to a more fulfilling existence.

The journey begins with a redefinition of wealth—one that transcends traditional notions and invites a broader perspective. It is not confined to the digits in our bank accounts but includes the richness of our experiences, the depth of our connections, and the impact we make on the world. This redefined concept of wealth becomes a powerful force, guiding us toward a life that is not only financially prosperous but also deeply satisfying on a personal and emotional level.

The Holistic Approach to Financial Abundance

As we delve into the heart of this exploration, we recognize that a fulfilling life is the result of a holistic approach to wealth. True prosperity is not achieved by compartmentalizing our financial goals from the rest of our aspirations. Instead, it involves integrating financial success with personal values, passions, and a sense of purpose.

This holistic perspective forms the foundation of "Beyond Riches." It's an invitation to consider wealth not as an isolated achievement but as an integral part of a fulfilling life. The chapters that follow will guide you through the intricacies of this approach, helping you weave together the threads of financial well-being, personal growth, and meaningful connections.

Cultivating a Mindset of Abundance

The journey to mastering wealth begins within the mind. A wealth mindset is not solely about accumulating wealth but understanding the possibilities that exist within and around us. In this section, we'll explore the power of positive thinking, overcoming limiting beliefs, and aligning our thoughts with the abundance that life has to offer. It's a shift in perspective that sets the stage for the practical strategies and insights that follow.

Aligning Wealth Goals with Personal Values

Central to the pursuit of a fulfilling life is the alignment of wealth goals with our deepest values. Wealth, when pursued in harmony with our values, becomes a force for good—an instrument to create positive change in our lives and the lives of others. This section will guide you in clarifying your values and integrating them into your financial journey, ensuring that your pursuit of wealth is not only successful but also meaningful.

As we embark on this journey "Beyond Riches," may you discover not only the pathways to financial prosperity but also the keys to a life that resonates with purpose, joy, and fulfillment. Join me as we uncover the transformative potential that lies within the intersection of wealth and a deeply satisfying life.

The Wealth Mindset

A. Cultivating a Mindset of Abundance

In the intricate tapestry of wealth mastery, the foundation lies within the recesses of the mind. Cultivating a mindset of abundance is the cornerstone upon which financial prosperity is built. It is not merely about accumulating wealth but fostering a profound understanding of the boundless opportunities that surround us.

Embracing Abundance

Abundance is a state of mind before it becomes a reality. In a world often perceived through the lens of scarcity, cultivating a mindset of abundance requires a conscious shift in perspective. It involves acknowledging that opportunities, resources, and possibilities are limitless. The mindset of abundance is not oblivious to challenges but chooses to focus on the vast potential for growth and success.

One powerful way to embrace abundance is through gratitude. By acknowledging and appreciating the resources, relationships, and experiences already present in our lives, we create a fertile ground for the seeds of wealth to flourish. Gratitude opens our eyes to the richness that surrounds us, paving the way for a mindset that attracts, rather than repels, prosperity.

The Power of Positive Thinking

Positive thinking is not merely a cliché; it is a force that shapes the contours of our reality. The thoughts we harbor influence our actions, decisions, and, ultimately, our outcomes. Cultivating a wealth mindset involves consciously choosing positive thoughts and beliefs about our financial journey.

Consider your thoughts as seeds planted in the fertile soil of your mind. Positive thoughts are seeds of potential that, when nurtured, grow into a garden of opportunities. In this section, we will explore practical strategies for fostering positive thinking, creating a mental environment that propels you towards your wealth goals.

Overcoming Limiting Beliefs

As we delve deeper into the wealth mindset, it becomes imperative to address the barriers that hinder its development—limiting beliefs. These are the deeply ingrained convictions about ourselves, money, and success that act as invisible chains, constraining our potential for financial abundance.

Identifying and Challenging Limiting Beliefs

Limiting beliefs often operate beneath the surface, shaping our attitudes and behaviors without our conscious awareness. In this section, we will embark on a journey of self-discovery, identifying the beliefs that may be holding you back. Once illuminated, we will delve into strategies for challenging and reframing these beliefs, unlocking the doors to untapped potential.

It's essential to recognize that overcoming limiting beliefs is not a one-time endeavor but an ongoing process of self-awareness and growth. By understanding the roots of these beliefs and consciously choosing empowering alternatives, you pave the way for a mindset that aligns with your wealth aspirations.

Embracing a Growth Mindset

At the heart of overcoming limiting beliefs is the cultivation of a growth mindset. Coined by psychologist Carol S. Dweck, a growth mindset is the belief that abilities and intelligence can be developed through dedication and hard work. In the context of wealth, this mindset shift opens the door to continuous learning, resilience in the face of challenges, and a willingness to embrace opportunities for growth.

Aligning Wealth Goals with Personal Values

As we navigate the intricate landscape of wealth, it's crucial to anchor our financial aspirations in a solid framework—our personal values. Aligning wealth goals with personal values not only lends purpose to our endeavors but also ensures that our pursuit of wealth is a harmonious journey rather than a disjointed pursuit of external markers of success.

Clarifying Your Core Values

Before setting specific wealth goals, take the time to clarify your core values. What principles guide your decisions, actions, and relationships? By understanding your values, you create a compass that directs your financial journey toward alignment with your authentic self.

Integrating Values into Financial Planning

Aligning wealth goals with personal values involves integrating these principles into your financial planning. This goes beyond numerical targets and delves into the qualitative aspects of your financial decisions. It's about ensuring that every step on your wealth journey resonates with your values, creating a sense of fulfillment and authenticity.

In this section, we will explore practical strategies for incorporating your values into financial goal-setting, decision-making, and long-term planning. By weaving your values into the fabric of your wealth journey, you not only enhance the meaningfulness of your achievements but also create a sustainable foundation for lasting fulfillment.

As we conclude this chapter, remember that cultivating a wealth mindset is not a destination but an ongoing practice. The principles explored here will serve as guideposts on your journey, empowering you to navigate the complexities of wealth with resilience, positivity, and a deep sense of purpose. In the chapters ahead, we will continue to build upon these foundations, unraveling the layers of wealth mastery for a fulfilling life.

Financial Education

Basics of Personal Finance

In the symphony of wealth creation, mastering the basics of personal finance serves as the foundational melody. Before delving into complex investment strategies or sophisticated financial instruments, it is crucial to establish a robust understanding of the fundamental principles that govern our financial lives.

Budgeting: The Cornerstone of Financial Stability

At the heart of personal finance lies the art of budgeting. This is not merely a restrictive ledger but a powerful tool that empowers individuals to take control of their financial destinies. In this section, we will explore the nuances of effective budgeting—allocating resources, managing expenses, and creating a roadmap for financial success.

Understanding your income, tracking expenses, and setting realistic financial goals form the essence of a well-crafted budget. We will delve into practical tips and strategies to create a budget that aligns with your lifestyle while paving the way for savings, investments, and the pursuit of your financial aspirations.

Emergency Funds and Financial Resilience

As we navigate the unpredictable currents of life, building financial resilience becomes paramount. Establishing emergency funds serves as a protective shield against unforeseen circumstances, providing a financial buffer in times of need. This section will guide you in creating and maintaining emergency funds, ensuring that you are prepared for unexpected twists on your wealth journey.

Investment Strategies for Sustainable Wealth

With a solid understanding of personal finance, the stage is set to explore the realm of investment strategies—an integral aspect of sustainable wealth creation. Beyond traditional savings, strategic investments are the engines that drive financial growth and prosperity.

Diversification and Risk Management

Successful investing is not about placing all your eggs in one basket; it's about diversification. This section will unravel the significance of spreading investments across different asset classes to mitigate risks and enhance overall portfolio performance. We will explore the art of balancing risk and reward, helping you craft an investment strategy that aligns with your financial goals and risk tolerance.

The Power of Compound Interest

Albert Einstein famously referred to compound interest as the eighth wonder of the world.

Understanding and harnessing the power of compound interest can significantly amplify the growth of your wealth over time. Whether you are just starting your investment journey or reassessing existing portfolios, this section will illuminate the principles of compound interest and its transformative impact on long-term wealth accumulation.

Realizing Returns in Real Estate

Real estate stands as a tangible and historically proven avenue for wealth creation. From rental properties to real estate investment trusts (REITs), this section will guide you through the intricacies of real estate investing. We will explore strategies for maximizing returns, navigating market fluctuations, and building a diversified real estate portfolio.

Continuous Learning and Adaptation

In the ever-evolving landscape of finance, stagnation is the enemy of wealth creation. Continuous learning and adaptation are not merely desirable; they are essential for staying ahead in a dynamic financial environment.

The Importance of Financial Literacy

Financial literacy is the compass that guides effective decision-making in the complex world of finance. This section emphasizes the significance of ongoing financial education, providing resources and insights to enhance your financial literacy. From understanding investment terminology to deciphering economic indicators, continuous learning forms the bedrock of financial empowerment.

Adapting to Changing Financial Landscapes

The financial world is marked by constant change—economic shifts, technological advancements, and global events shape the terrain on which financial decisions are made. This section will explore strategies for adapting to changing financial landscapes. From embracing technological innovations in fintech to navigating economic downturns, we will equip you with the tools to thrive in an ever-changing financial ecosystem.

As we conclude this chapter on financial education, remember that knowledge is not static; it is a dynamic force that empowers you to make informed decisions and navigate the complexities of wealth creation. The principles and strategies explored here will serve as a compass on your financial journey, guiding you towards sustainable wealth and financial mastery. In the chapters that follow, we will delve deeper into the layers of wealth creation, building upon the solid foundation of financial education.

Income Diversification

Building Multiple Streams of Income

In the intricate dance of wealth creation, the concept of income diversification emerges as a powerful rhythm that orchestrates financial harmony. Building multiple streams of income is not just a strategy; it's a paradigm shift that transforms the traditional notion of relying solely on a single source of revenue.

The Paradigm Shift: Beyond a Single Income Source

Traditionally, many individuals have relied on a singular income source, often tied to employment. However, the landscape of work and wealth is evolving, and the concept of financial security is no longer synonymous with a single paycheck. This section will explore the advantages of diversifying your income streams, ranging from increased financial stability to the flexibility to pursue diverse opportunities.

Exploring Different Income Streams

Building multiple income streams involves strategic planning and a willingness to explore various avenues. From passive income through investments to active income from side hustles or freelancing, we will delve into the myriad options available. Uncover the potential of dividends, royalties, and other income sources that can work synergistically to create a robust financial foundation.

Balancing Risk and Reward

While the benefits of income diversification are evident, it's crucial to strike a balance between risk and reward. Not all income streams are created equal, and understanding the risk profile of each is paramount. This section will guide you in evaluating and diversifying your income streams intelligently, ensuring a resilient financial portfolio.

Entrepreneurial Ventures and Wealth Creation

Entrepreneurship stands as a beacon for those seeking not just financial success but the fulfillment of their creative and innovative aspirations. In this section, we explore how entrepreneurial ventures can become dynamic catalysts for wealth creation.

The Entrepreneurial Mindset

Embarking on entrepreneurial ventures involves more than launching a business; it requires adopting an entrepreneurial mindset. This mindset is characterized by innovation, resilience, and a willingness to take calculated risks. We will delve into the key attributes of the entrepreneurial mindset and how cultivating it can fuel your journey toward financial abundance.

Navigating Entrepreneurial Challenges

Entrepreneurship is not without its challenges, and this section will provide insights into navigating the common hurdles encountered on the entrepreneurial path. From managing uncertainty to building a resilient business model, you'll gain strategies for overcoming obstacles and steering your venture toward sustainable success.

Scaling and Diversifying Business Ventures

Beyond the inception of a business, scaling and diversifying ventures are pivotal steps toward long-term wealth creation. This section will explore strategies for scaling your business operations and diversifying your product or service offerings. Discover how expansion and diversification can amplify your entrepreneurial impact and contribute to lasting financial prosperity.

Advancing Careers Strategically for Financial Growth

For many individuals, career advancement serves as a primary avenue for financial growth. In this section, we explore strategic approaches to advancing your career and leveraging professional opportunities for increased income.

Strategic Career Development

Advancing your career requires a strategic approach that goes beyond day-to-day tasks. This section will guide you through the principles of strategic career development, emphasizing the importance of continuous learning, networking, and positioning yourself for growth within your chosen field.

Negotiating for Financial Success

Effective negotiation skills are paramount in achieving financial growth within a professional context. Whether negotiating a salary, benefits package, or project terms, this section will provide practical tips for mastering the art of negotiation. Learn how to confidently articulate your value and secure favorable terms that contribute to your financial well-being.

Investing in Professional Development

In a rapidly evolving job market, investing in your professional development is an investment in your financial future. This section will explore the value of ongoing education, skill development, and certifications in enhancing your career trajectory. Discover how staying ahead of industry trends and acquiring new skills can open doors to higher-paying opportunities.

As we navigate the realm of income diversification, entrepreneurship, and strategic career advancement, remember that wealth creation is a dynamic and multifaceted journey. The principles and strategies explored in this chapter are designed to empower you to diversify your income sources intelligently, harness the entrepreneurial spirit for wealth creation, and strategically advance your career for lasting financial growth. In the chapters that follow, we will continue to unravel the layers of wealth mastery, building upon the diversified foundation established in this chapter.

Strategic Money Management

Budgeting for Success

In the symphony of wealth creation, the conductor of financial harmony is undoubtedly budgeting. Far from being a restrictive regimen, effective budgeting serves as a dynamic tool that empowers individuals to orchestrate their financial future. As we embark on this exploration of strategic money management, let's delve into the nuances of budgeting for success.

The Art of Budgeting

At its core, budgeting is the intentional allocation of resources to achieve financial goals. It's not about constraining your lifestyle but about aligning your spending with your priorities. In this section, we will unravel the art of budgeting—creating a roadmap that balances income, expenses, and savings.

Goal-Centric Budgeting

One of the key principles of effective budgeting is aligning your financial decisions with your goals. Whether it's saving for a home, building an emergency fund, or investing for retirement, a goal-centric budget ensures that every dollar serves a purpose. We will explore practical strategies for identifying and prioritizing your financial goals, creating a customized budget that propels you toward success.

Tracking and Adjusting

The journey to financial success is not a one-time event but an ongoing process of refinement. Tracking your spending and regularly adjusting your budget are essential components of strategic money management. Discover tools and techniques to monitor your financial habits, identify areas for improvement, and make proactive adjustments to stay on course.

Effective Saving and Investing

With a well-crafted budget in place, the next movements in the symphony of strategic money management involve effective saving and investing.

These components are not merely about accumulating wealth; they are about nurturing and growing the financial seeds planted through intentional budgeting.

The Power of Systematic Saving

Saving is not just a habit; it's a financial superpower. This section will explore the principles of systematic saving, including the importance of emergency funds, short-term savings, and long-term investment goals. Uncover strategies for automating your saving process and cultivating a mindset that values delayed gratification for lasting financial success.

Investment Strategies for Wealth Accumulation

Investing is the engine that propels your wealth journey forward. From stocks and bonds to real estate and retirement accounts, this section will guide you through effective investment strategies. Understand the risk-return relationship, explore different investment vehicles, and gain insights into creating a diversified investment portfolio aligned with your financial goals.

Harnessing the Benefits of Compound Growth

As we explore effective saving and investing, the concept of compound growth emerges as a powerful force. Einstein referred to compound interest as the eighth wonder of the world, and understanding its dynamics is key to maximizing your wealth over time. Learn how compounding works and how it amplifies the growth of your savings and investments, creating a snowball effect that contributes to long-term prosperity.

Debt Management for Long-Term Prosperity

While saving and investing are essential elements of wealth creation, effective debt management serves as a stabilizing force, ensuring that your financial foundation remains robust. In this section, we will explore strategies for navigating debt wisely and positioning yourself for long-term prosperity.

Understanding and Evaluating Debt

Debt, when managed strategically, can be a tool for financial growth. This section will guide you in understanding the different types of debt, evaluating their impact on your financial health, and distinguishing between "good" and "bad" debt. Gain insights into making informed decisions about taking on debt and leveraging it to your advantage.

Creating a Debt Repayment Plan

If you find yourself with existing debt, developing a structured repayment plan is crucial. Whether it's student loans, credit card debt, or a mortgage, this section will provide actionable steps for creating a debt repayment strategy. Explore methods such as the debt snowball and debt avalanche, and discover which approach aligns best with your financial situation.

Building a Debt-Free Future

Ultimately, the goal of debt management is not just repayment but achieving a debt-free future. This section will guide you through the steps to build a solid financial foundation, free from the burden of excessive debt. Learn how to prevent future debt accumulation, cultivate financial discipline, and position yourself for lasting prosperity.

As we conclude this chapter on strategic money management, remember that it is not a rigid set of rules but a flexible framework designed to adapt to your unique financial journey. The principles explored here—the art of budgeting, effective saving and investing, and wise debt management—lay the groundwork for a resilient and prosperous financial future. In the chapters that follow, we will continue to unravel the layers of wealth mastery, building upon the strategic foundation established in this chapter.

Realizing Wealth through Real Estate

Fundamentals of Real Estate Investment

In the realm of wealth creation, real estate stands as an enduring and tangible asset class that has shaped the financial destinies of many. Understanding the fundamentals of real estate investment is not just a strategic choice; it's a journey into a world where properties become pathways to lasting prosperity.

The Unique Appeal of Real Estate

Real estate possesses a unique appeal, offering both stability and the potential for substantial returns. This section will delve into the reasons behind the allure of real estate as an investment. From its capacity to generate passive income through rentals to the potential for property value appreciation, discover why real estate holds a prominent place in the wealth-building toolkit.

Types of Real Estate Investments

Real estate is a vast landscape, and navigating it requires an understanding of different investment types. Residential properties, commercial real estate, and real estate investment trusts (REITs) are just a few examples. Explore the characteristics, advantages, and considerations of each, gaining insights into how they align with your financial goals and risk tolerance.

Conducting Due Diligence in Real Estate

One of the pillars of successful real estate investment is thorough due diligence. This involves researching and evaluating potential properties, understanding market dynamics, and assessing potential risks. Uncover the key aspects of due diligence, from analyzing property values to assessing the economic indicators that impact real estate markets.

Maximizing Returns and Minimizing Risks

While the potential for wealth creation in real estate is significant, so too are the risks. Maximizing returns and minimizing risks require a strategic approach that combines market insight, financial acumen, and a commitment to informed decision-making.

Strategic Property Selection

Choosing the right property is foundational to real estate success. This section will guide you through the considerations for strategic property selection. From location analysis to evaluating property condition, discover the factors that contribute to a wise investment decision. Learn how to identify properties with the potential for value appreciation and rental income.

Financing Strategies for Real Estate

Real estate investments often involve substantial capital, and navigating financing options is a crucial aspect of maximizing returns. Explore different financing strategies, from traditional mortgages to creative financing solutions. Understand how leveraging can amplify returns while managing financial risks responsibly.

Risk Mitigation in Real Estate

Real estate, like any investment, carries inherent risks. Successful investors are adept at identifying and mitigating these risks. This section will explore risk management strategies specific to real estate. From diversifying your real estate portfolio to having contingency plans for market fluctuations, learn how to navigate challenges while safeguarding your wealth.

Building Wealth through Property Ownership

Property ownership extends beyond the realm of investment; it is a tangible manifestation of wealth creation. Whether acquiring a home for personal use or building a portfolio of rental properties, the journey of building wealth through property ownership involves both strategic decisions and a long-term vision.

Homeownership as a Wealth-Building Tool

For many, homeownership is a significant milestone and a cornerstone of wealth creation. This section will explore how owning a home can contribute to long-term financial stability and act as a form of forced savings. Understand the financial benefits of homeownership, from potential property appreciation to tax advantages.

Creating Passive Income with Rental Properties

Rental properties are a potent avenue for creating passive income streams. This section will guide you through the process of building wealth through rental property ownership. From selecting rental properties strategically to managing tenants effectively, uncover the keys to generating consistent income while building equity.

Real Estate as a Legacy-Building Tool

Beyond the immediate benefits, real estate can serve as a tool for building a lasting legacy. Whether passing down properties to future generations or using real estate as a vehicle for charitable contributions, this section will explore how real estate ownership can transcend individual wealth creation and contribute to a meaningful legacy.

As we conclude this chapter on realizing wealth through real estate, remember that real estate investment is both an art and a science. The principles explored here—the fundamentals of real estate investment, maximizing returns while minimizing risks, and building wealth through property ownership—

provide a comprehensive framework for navigating the complexities of the real estate landscape. In the chapters that follow, we will continue to unravel the layers of wealth mastery, building upon the insights and strategies established in this exploration of real estate wealth creation.

Planning for the Future

Retirement Strategies for Lasting Prosperity

In the symphony of wealth creation, orchestrating a harmonious retirement is a movement that requires careful planning and strategic foresight. Retirement is not just a culmination of a professional journey; it marks the transition into a phase where financial security and lasting prosperity become paramount.

Understanding the Importance of Retirement Planning

Retirement planning is not merely a financial task; it's a comprehensive strategy that spans lifestyle considerations, healthcare needs, and the pursuit of lifelong aspirations. This section will explore why retirement planning is a cornerstone of lasting prosperity, emphasizing the significance of proactive preparation for the golden years.

Financial Aspects of Retirement Planning

The financial aspects of retirement planning involve a delicate balance of saving, investing, and creating a sustainable income stream. From understanding pension plans to maximizing contributions to retirement accounts, this section will guide you through the key financial considerations. Uncover strategies for estimating your retirement needs, optimizing your savings, and creating a retirement portfolio that withstands the test of time.

Lifestyle and Health Considerations in Retirement

Retirement is not just about financial security; it's about designing a lifestyle that aligns with your aspirations. This section will delve into lifestyle considerations, including choosing a retirement location, planning for travel, and pursuing hobbies and passions. Additionally, we will explore healthcare considerations and strategies for maintaining physical and mental well-being during retirement.

Legacy Building and Generational Wealth

The desire to leave a lasting legacy transcends financial success; it involves imparting a meaningful impact on future generations. Legacy building and generational wealth go hand in hand, creating a narrative that extends beyond individual achievements to a collective family story of prosperity.

Defining Your Legacy

Legacy is not confined to financial assets; it encompasses values, traditions, and the impact we make on the world. This section will guide you in defining your legacy—clarifying the principles and ideals you wish to pass down to future generations. Explore strategies for integrating your values into family discussions and creating a roadmap for building a meaningful legacy.

Generational Wealth Strategies

Generational wealth is about creating a financial foundation that supports not only the present but also future generations. From education funds to investment structures that span multiple generations, this section will explore strategies for building and preserving wealth over time. Discover how to create a family wealth plan that ensures your financial legacy endures for generations to come.

Nurturing Financial Education in the Family

A key element of generational wealth is fostering financial education within the family. This section will provide insights into how to cultivate a mindset of financial responsibility and literacy among family members. Explore age-appropriate financial education strategies, from teaching basic money management skills to involving family members in financial decision-making.

Estate Planning for a Smooth Wealth Transition

Estate planning is the final movement in the symphony of planning for the future. It involves not only the distribution of assets but also the seamless transition of wealth to heirs. A well-crafted estate plan ensures that your wealth continues to serve its intended purposes and that your legacy endures.

The Essentials of Estate Planning

Estate planning involves a comprehensive review of your assets, creating legal documents, and designating beneficiaries. This section will guide you through the essentials of estate planning, from creating a will to establishing trusts. Understand the importance of powers of attorney, healthcare directives, and other documents that ensure your wishes are honored in the event of incapacity or death.

Minimizing Estate Taxes

Effective estate planning also involves strategies to minimize tax implications on your estate. Explore tactics for maximizing exemptions, utilizing trusts, and implementing gifting strategies to reduce the impact of estate taxes. By taking a proactive approach, you can preserve more of your wealth for future generations.

Facilitating a Smooth Wealth Transition

Ensuring a smooth wealth transition involves open communication, clarity in your wishes, and the appointment of capable individuals to manage your affairs. This section will provide guidance on facilitating conversations with heirs, selecting trustworthy executors, and preparing the next generation for their roles in managing family wealth. Learn how to create a roadmap that streamlines the transition of wealth, reducing potential conflicts and ensuring a legacy of financial prosperity.

As we conclude this chapter on planning for the future, remember that the choices you make today ripple through time, shaping not only your future but also the legacy you leave behind. The principles explored here— the importance of retirement planning, legacy building and generational wealth, and effective estate planning—provide a roadmap for a future that is not only financially secure but also meaningful and enduring. In the chapters that follow, we will continue to unravel the layers of wealth mastery, building upon the strategic insights and foresight established in this exploration of future planning.

Navigating Economic Challenges

Resilience in Economic Downturns

In the dynamic landscape of wealth creation, economic downturns are inevitable ripples that test the resilience of financial strategies. Navigating economic challenges requires not only an understanding of market dynamics but also the cultivation of a resilient mindset that can weather the storms of uncertainty.

Embracing a Resilient Mindset

Resilience in economic downturns begins with a mindset that reframes challenges as opportunities for growth. This section will explore the characteristics of a resilient mindset—adapting to change, maintaining a long-term perspective, and leveraging setbacks as stepping stones to future success. Discover how embracing adversity can lead to not only financial survival but also thriving in the face of economic challenges.

Building a Robust Financial Safety Net

Preparation is a cornerstone of resilience, and having a robust financial safety net is essential during economic downturns. From emergency funds to contingency plans, this section will guide you in building a financial cushion that acts as a shield against unforeseen challenges. Explore strategies for conservatively managing debt, securing liquidity, and positioning your financial portfolio to withstand economic turbulence.

Strategizing for Economic Recovery

While economic downturns bring challenges, they also create opportunities for strategic positioning. This section will explore strategies for not only weathering economic storms but also capitalizing on recovery. From identifying undervalued assets to adapting investment strategies, learn how to position yourself for resilience and growth during periods of economic uncertainty.

Risk Management in Investments

Investing inherently involves risk, and understanding how to manage and mitigate risks is a fundamental aspect of wealth creation. Whether you're a seasoned investor or just starting, effective risk management is a skill that can significantly impact the longevity and success of your investment portfolio.

Evaluating and Understanding Investment Risks

Risk management begins with a thorough evaluation and understanding of the risks associated with different investments. This section will guide you through the common types of investment risks, from market volatility to specific industry risks. Gain insights into conducting risk assessments and aligning your investment strategy with your risk tolerance and financial goals.

Diversification as a Risk Mitigation Strategy

Diversification is a powerful tool in managing investment risks. This section will delve into the principles of diversification—spreading investments across different asset classes, industries, and geographic regions. Discover how diversification can reduce the impact of individual investment fluctuations and contribute to a more resilient and balanced portfolio.

Monitoring and Adjusting Investment Strategies

Effective risk management is an ongoing process that involves monitoring and adjusting investment strategies in response to changing market conditions. This section will explore how to stay informed about market trends, economic indicators, and global events that may impact your investments. Learn when and how to adjust your portfolio to proactively manage risks and seize opportunities.

Adapting to Changing Financial Landscapes

The financial world is dynamic, shaped by technological advancements, global events, and evolving economic landscapes. Adapting to changing financial landscapes is not just a skill; it's a necessity for those seeking enduring success in wealth creation.

Embracing Technological Innovations

Technology has revolutionized the financial industry, from online banking to robo-advisors and blockchain. This section will explore the impact of technological innovations on personal finance and investing. Understand how to leverage technology to streamline financial management, stay informed about market trends, and embrace innovations that can enhance your financial strategies.

The Role of Education in Adaptation

Adapting to changing financial landscapes requires continuous learning and staying informed about industry trends. This section will emphasize the importance of ongoing financial education. From online courses to staying updated on economic news, discover how investing in your financial knowledge equips you with the tools t I'mo navigate evolving financial terrains.

Flexibility in Financial Planning

Rigid financial plans may struggle to withstand the dynamics of changing landscapes. This section will explore the importance of flexibility in financial planning. Learn how to adapt your financial goals and strategies in response to shifts in economic conditions, ensuring that your plans remain relevant and effective.

Seeking Professional Guidance

In times of uncertainty and rapid change, seeking professional guidance becomes invaluable. This section will discuss the role of financial advisors in navigating changing financial landscapes. Explore how a qualified advisor can provide insights, recommend strategic adjustments, and offer a steady hand during economic turbulence. Understand the value of building a collaborative relationship with financial professionals who can contribute to your long-term financial success.

As we conclude this chapter on navigating economic challenges, remember that resilience, effective risk management, and adaptability are pillars that support enduring financial success. The principles explored here provide a comprehensive framework for not only surviving economic challenges but thriving in the midst of uncertainty. In the chapters that follow, we will continue to unravel the layers of wealth mastery, building upon the insights and strategies established in this exploration of navigating economic challenges.

Balancing Wealth and Well-Being

The Intersection of Wealth and Health

In the intricate tapestry of life, the pursuit of wealth often intertwines with the quest for well-being. As we delve into the exploration of balancing wealth and well-being, it's essential to recognize the profound connection between financial prosperity and physical, mental, and emotional health.

Understanding the Relationship Between Wealth and Health

Wealth and health share a symbiotic relationship that goes beyond mere coincidence. This section will explore the ways in which financial well-being can impact physical health. From access to quality healthcare to the ability to make lifestyle choices that promote wellness, discover how wealth can serve as a catalyst for a healthier and more fulfilling life.

Mitigating the Stressors of Wealth

While wealth brings numerous advantages, it also introduces its own set of stressors. Balancing financial responsibilities, managing investments, and navigating complex financial decisions can contribute to stress. This section will delve into strategies for mitigating the stressors of wealth, from effective financial planning to cultivating mindfulness practices that promote emotional well-being.

Investing in Health as a Form of Wealth

Health is not just an outcome of wealth; it is an essential component of wealth itself. This section will explore the concept of investing in health as a form of wealth. Understand how prioritizing physical and mental well-being contributes to longevity, enhances quality of life, and ultimately strengthens the foundation for enduring financial success.

Relationships and Fulfillment Beyond Financial Success

Wealth, when viewed holistically, extends beyond monetary abundance to encompass the richness of relationships and personal fulfillment. This section will illuminate the importance of nurturing meaningful connections and finding fulfillment beyond the realm of financial success.

The Role of Relationships in Well-Being

Quality relationships are a cornerstone of overall well-being. This section will explore the impact of relationships on mental and emotional health. From family bonds to friendships and romantic connections, discover how cultivating and maintaining positive relationships contributes to a more fulfilling and balanced life.

Balancing Professional Success with Personal Fulfillment

The pursuit of professional success is often a driving force in wealth creation, but it's crucial to strike a balance with personal fulfillment. This section will guide you in navigating the intersection of professional achievement and personal well-being. Explore strategies for aligning career goals with your values, setting boundaries, and fostering a sense of purpose that transcends monetary success.

Finding Fulfillment in Non-Material Pursuits

Beyond the tangible markers of wealth, true fulfillment often lies in non-material pursuits. This section will explore the role of hobbies, passions, and philanthropy in enhancing overall well-being. Understand how engaging in activities that bring joy and purpose contributes to a more balanced and satisfying life.

Mindfulness Practices for a Balanced Life

Mindfulness, the practice of being fully present in the moment, emerges as a powerful tool for achieving balance in the intersection of wealth and well-being. This section will delve into mindfulness practices that promote mental clarity, emotional resilience, and a sense of equilibrium.

The Power of Mindfulness in Financial Decision-Making

Mindfulness is not confined to meditation; it extends to the realm of financial decision-making. This section will explore how cultivating mindfulness can enhance your ability to make thoughtful and strategic financial choices. From avoiding impulsive decisions to managing financial stress, discover how a mindful approach can lead to more informed and intentional wealth-related actions.

Integrating Mindfulness into Daily Life

Mindfulness is a practice that extends beyond specific moments of meditation. This section will provide practical tips for integrating mindfulness into your daily life. From mindful eating to incorporating moments of reflection into your routine, learn how to infuse your everyday activities with a sense of presence and awareness.

Achieving Balance: Mindfulness and Financial Success

Achieving balance between wealth and well-being involves recognizing the interconnectedness of the two realms. This section will explore how mindfulness can be a catalyst for achieving that balance. Understand how mindfulness practices contribute to stress reduction, enhance decision-making, and foster a holistic approach to wealth that prioritizes overall well-being.

As we navigate the intersection of wealth and well-being, remember that true prosperity encompasses more than financial success; it embraces health, relationships, and a sense of fulfillment. The principles explored in this chapter provide a holistic perspective on wealth, guiding you toward a balanced and meaningful life. In the chapters that follow, we will continue to unravel the layers of wealth mastery, building upon the insights and practices established in this exploration of balancing wealth and well-being.

Conclusion

Recap and Key Takeaways

As we conclude this comprehensive journey through the realms of wealth creation, financial mastery, and the intricate interplay of prosperity and well-being, it's essential to reflect on the key insights and takeaways that form the foundation of a fulfilling and wealthy life.

Navigating the Wealth Landscape

We embarked on this journey with the premise that wealth creation is not a linear path but a dynamic and multifaceted landscape. From the fundamentals of financial literacy to the intricacies of real estate investment, retirement planning, and navigating economic challenges, each chapter unfolded layers of knowledge and strategies.

The Holistic Nature of Wealth

Throughout our exploration, a central theme emerged—the holistic nature of wealth. True prosperity extends beyond monetary abundance to encompass health, relationships, mindfulness, and a sense of purpose. The intersection of wealth and well-being became a focal point, emphasizing that lasting success involves a delicate balance across various facets of life.

Building a Foundation of Financial Education

At the core of wealth creation lies financial education. Understanding the basics of personal finance, investment strategies, and risk management serves as the bedrock for informed decision-making. Whether you are just starting your financial journey or seeking to enhance your existing knowledge, continuous learning remains a key principle for financial empowerment.

Crafting a Strategic Financial Plan

Crafting a strategic financial plan emerged as a crucial step in the wealth creation process. From budgeting and saving to investing and debt management, a well-thought-out plan provides the roadmap for achieving financial goals. The principles of diversification, risk mitigation, and adaptability were underscored as essential components of a resilient financial strategy.

Balancing Wealth and Well-Being

As we explored the intricate dance between wealth and well-being, the importance of balance became evident. Nurturing relationships, finding fulfillment beyond material success, and integrating mindfulness practices contribute to a more holistic and meaningful life. The chapter on balancing wealth and well-being served as a reminder that true prosperity encompasses not only financial success but also overall well-being.

Empowering Readers for a Fulfilling and Wealthy Life

Empowering readers for a fulfilling and wealthy life involves more than imparting knowledge; it requires instilling a mindset of continuous growth, adaptability, and purpose. As we wrap up this journey, let's delve into the empowering principles that serve as a beacon for readers seeking enduring prosperity.

Cultivating a Growth Mindset

A growth mindset forms the foundation of empowerment. Embracing challenges, viewing failures as opportunities to learn, and consistently seeking improvement are hallmarks of a growth-oriented mindset. As you navigate the complexities of wealth creation, approach each obstacle as a chance for growth and refinement.

Fostering Adaptability in Financial Strategies

The financial landscape is dynamic, marked by constant change and evolving trends. Empowerment in wealth creation involves fostering adaptability in your financial strategies. Stay informed about industry shifts, be open to adjusting your plans, and embrace innovation in financial technologies. A willingness to adapt positions you for success in the ever-changing economic terrain.

Prioritizing Well-Being Alongside Wealth

True empowerment involves recognizing the interconnectedness of wealth and well-being. Prioritize your physical, mental, and emotional health as integral components of your wealth. Cultivate meaningful relationships, engage in activities that bring joy, and incorporate mindfulness practices into your daily life. Well-being not only enhances the quality of your life but also contributes to sustained success in your financial journey.

Embracing a Purpose-Driven Approach

Beyond financial metrics, a purpose-driven approach amplifies the meaning and impact of your wealth creation journey. Define your values, aspirations, and the legacy you wish to leave behind. Align your financial goals with a deeper sense of purpose, allowing your wealth to serve as a tool for positive impact and lasting fulfillment.

Inspiring Ongoing Financial Education

Empowerment is a continuous journey, and ongoing financial education is the compass that guides you through the complexities of wealth creation. Stay curious, seek out new knowledge, and embrace opportunities for learning. Whether through books, courses, or networking with financial professionals, the pursuit of knowledge remains a powerful driver of empowerment.

Conclusion: A Call to Action

As we close the final chapter of this exploration into wealth mastery, let it serve as a call to action. The knowledge, insights, and empowering principles shared throughout this journey are not mere concepts but tools for you to wield in crafting a fulfilling and wealthy life.

Remember that wealth creation is a dynamic and evolving process. Embrace the challenges, celebrate the victories, and remain committed to your financial and personal growth. You hold the pen to your financial narrative, and each decision you make shapes the chapters of your wealth journey.

May this comprehensive exploration be a guiding light on your path to enduring prosperity. Whether you are just beginning your wealth creation journey or seeking to elevate your strategies, let the principles of financial education, strategic planning, and holistic well-being empower you to navigate the ever-changing landscape of wealth.

As you turn the page from this conclusion, carry with you the empowerment to shape a life that transcends monetary success—a life rich in purpose, balanced in well-being, and abundant in